"Your work needs a new story. Thi_ Work_ compels us to consider. Drawin_ story, common cultural distortions a and gracefully swept away. A clarifyin_ _ _s to embrace the life-giving rhythms of a seamles_ _ _ of living into our daily work. Whether you enjoy your work or are struggling with it, this well-crafted and practical book will help you discover how faith shapes and brings meaning to your Monday world. I recommend it."

Tom Nelson, president of Made to Flourish and senior pastor of Christ Community Church, Kansas City

"In this short but essential primer, Ross Chapman and Ryan Tafilowski have created a down-to-earth guide to understanding God's view of work, which is meant to play a redemptive role in a broken world and in our individual lives. This book has helped me look at my own work—both the paid and unpaid varieties—in a new and hopeful light."

Angie Ward, associate professor of leadership and ministry at Denver Seminary, and author of *I Am a Leader: When Women Discover the Joy of Their Calling*

"Grounding their argument in the mission of God, vocation and calling, and even political theology, Ross Chapman and Ryan Tafilowski speak to our deepest longings to participate in God's holistic, redemptive activity and to love our neighbor. They inspire our imaginations with a call to see daily work as intrinsically valuable, missionally focused, life giving, and transformational. Embracing the theology of work the authors carefully unpack in this book will lead to new joy in our daily work, new vision for its purpose in the world, and new hope in its capacity to contribute to the flourishing of all. This is a must-read."

Patty Pell, assistant professor of theology, justice, and social advocacy at Denver Seminary

"*Faithful Work* is succinct and well written, and deeply grounded in theology. The authors account for the realistic tensions of living in an increasingly pluralistic and polarized culture yet offer a hopeful account of how our work can participate in the redemption of all things. It is an extremely helpful guide for those looking to connect their faith with their work."

Kenman Wong, professor at Seattle Pacific University and coauthor of *Business for the Common Good: A Christian Vision for the Marketplace*

"*Faithful Work* is a helpful primer for those seeking to lay the foundation of their work on the right Cornerstone. This succinct, accessible manual replaces common, erroneous thinking, such as the sacred/secular divide, with a perspective of God's seamlessness. It calls us to perform good work in the places where God has called us and inspires us to work made intrinsically good because God works. *Faithful Work* maintains a foot in the reality of working in the world as it is, not as we wish it were, and leaves us with an important question: What if our daily work is the central place where the church embodies the gospel in daily living?"

Barry Rowan, author of *The Spiritual Art of Business* and former C-suite executive for four public companies

"*Faithful Work* encourages us to make our prayer for the manifestation of God's kingdom consistent with the practice of doing redemptive work. The book is full of pertinent and practical insights that can be applied by workers in any occupation and will help readers make their work more meaningful."

Shundrawn A. Thomas, author of *Discover Joy in Work: Transforming Your Occupation into Your Vocation*

"Ross Chapman and Ryan Tafilowski offer a theologically sound and biblically rich guide for our work, something we all need. I highly recommend *Faithful Work* to anyone who is looking for a compelling vision for their work."

David Spickard, founder and CEO of 11 Ten Leadership

"With refreshing brevity, biblical wisdom, and consistent attention to the daily grind of work, *Faithful Work* invites Christians to see their work as an essential element of God's redemptive activity. This book is perfect for all workers who are eager to find deeper meaning and purpose in their daily work. It would also be an effective discussion starter for small groups, adult classes, and faith-based employee resource groups. *Faithful Work* inspires us with the bold claim that 'our greatest opportunity is daily work.'"

Mark D. Roberts, senior strategist for Max De Pree Center for Leadership

Faithful

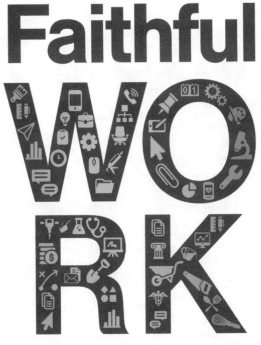

WORK

Ross Chapman
Ryan Tafilowski

In the Daily
Grind with God
and for Others

An imprint of InterVarsity Press
Downers Grove, Illinois

InterVarsity Press
P.O. Box 1400 | Downers Grove, IL 60515-1426
ivpress.com | email@ivpress.com

InterVarsity Press® is the publishing division of InterVarsity Christian Fellowship/USA®. For more information, visit intervarsity.org.

All Scripture quotations, unless otherwise indicated, are taken from The Holy Bible, New International Version®, NIV®. Copyright © 1973, 1978, 1984, 2011 by Biblica, Inc.™ Used by permission of Zondervan. All rights reserved worldwide. www.zondervan.com. The "NIV" and "New International Version" are trademarks registered in the United States Patent and Trademark Office by Biblica, Inc.™

While any stories in this book are true, some names and identifying information may have been changed to protect the privacy of individuals.

The publisher cannot verify the accuracy or functionality of website URLs used in this book beyond the date of publication.

Cover design: David Fassett
Interior design: Jeanna Wiggins
Cover images: Getty images: © -VICTOR-, © browndogstudios, © justinroque, © rambo182, © mikimad, © FloWBo, © bounward, © appleuzr, © Mironov Konstantin, Noun Project

ISBN 978-1-5140-0791-4 (print) | ISBN 978-1-5140-0792-1 (digital)

Printed in the United States of America ♾

Library of Congress Cataloging-in-Publication Data
A catalog record for this book is available from the Library of Congress.

30   29   28   27   26   25   24 | 8   7   6   5   4   3   2   1

ROSS—

To Candace and William, Pierce, and Beckett

May you always be able to see how your work

can be done with God and for others

RYAN—

To Bill and Penni Van Horn

Contents

INTRODUCTION:
Our Greatest Opportunity Is Daily Work   1

1. The Importance of Work   9

2. The Real Story of Work, in Short   21

3. Created and Placed by God for Good Work   33

4. The Reality of Work and Calling   43

5. Work in a Politicized and Polarized Society   53

6. Monday Through Saturday Missionaries   61

7. Rest for and in the Working   69

EPILOGUE: A Framework for Change   81

ACKNOWLEDGMENTS   91

NOTES   93

FURTHER READING   97

Our Greatest Opportunity Is Daily Work

S. TRUETT CATHY, the founder of Chick-fil-A, said, "Food is essential to life; therefore, make it good."

It's a fixture quote at Chick-fil-A restaurants now, but it's more than a motto. Cathy's Christian faith turned this statement into a charge to love one's neighbor with excellence. The fast-food restaurants make food good. Millions now have the exceptional option of enjoying the chicken sandwich any time they want.

They also made work good. Their customer service is consistently ranked the highest among all fast-food restaurants.[1] The product (food) *and* the process (customer service) are a direct result of how a biblical view of work changes the why, what, and how of daily work.

I (Ross Chapman) want to propose we can make the same statement about work: work is essential to life; therefore, make it good.

What we hope you'll find in this book is that these two parts of the statement above are a simple way to sum up what God, through Scripture, says about work.

Would anyone argue work is not essential to life?

Our organization's hometown, Denver, is a city often trying to work as little as possible to make more time for play, yet even this city would say work is essential. Flexible work that pays well is highly sought after because it enables play, whether it's winter sports in the Rocky Mountains, biking the many trails and streets of Denver, or enjoying evening entertainment and food.

Work, then, is essential because it's the thing that allows me to have a more desired thing. It's the means to a self-determined end.

That self-determined end may not be about skiing, hiking, or nightlife for you. Maybe it's more financial resources to live comfortably or take a big vacation. Maybe it's working enough to go on cruise control during retirement. Maybe it's what has to be done to pay the bills.

Maybe it's what brings a preferred status among peers and family members. Maybe it's just the rhythm and routine society has created as an attempt to keep things running and progressing.

There is no escaping work, it seems. Work really is essential to life. But it's essential for much bigger reasons than the ones we've just covered.

Often in our local communities of faith, the story of work is untold or limited to an instrumental understanding of it, meaning our everyday work can only be a means to something more important. And that something is typically determined by us or our spiritual leaders. Countless faithful churchgoers have gotten the message their daily work is mostly about two things: (1) providing financially for the work of the church as expressed through church-led ministries, nonprofits, and missionaries, and (2) evangelism. Sometimes work is not even given an instrumental value; rather it is perceived as getting in the way of "spiritual" activities.

Many factors contribute to low views of work—views that are limited, narrow, or negative; we'll explore some of them in this short book. But that's not the story of work in Scripture. Scripture has a very high view of work.

The first thing God tells us about himself is that he is a God who works. "In the beginning God created" (Genesis 1:1). Or said another way, God worked. Out of nothing, he made the universe and everything in it. That's more work than one person or all of humanity together can even imagine. And it's better work than we can imagine too. God likes work and he enjoys work, so much so that it is the first thing he tells us about himself.

Of course, God also had a purpose in the work he did—a self-determined one. But it's one thing for *God* to have an instrumental view of work, because he is true, just, and wholly good; it's quite another thing for *humanity* to have a self-determined view, because humanity is not wholly good, just, and true.

Throughout this book, we'll briefly explore God's work and humanity's work, and how God intended them to complement each other.

It was his plan from the beginning that our daily work would come alongside and submit to his work and purposes. Our work adds to his work. When we do our daily work out of who he intended us to be—his image bearers given the responsibility of bringing fruitfulness to his creation—we experience a taste of what it really means to be human, to live life to the full.

The origin story of work is good, exciting, and empowering. It's a message about the dignity and purpose of all the daily work of humanity, not just what we consider spiritual or sacred work.

But our everyday experience of work is broken.

Sometimes, work is just hard and frustrating. Results do not reflect the effort given. Bad work is rewarded and good work is ignored. Systems create winners and losers. Abuses of power, injustice, and poor or evil products abound in our daily work experience. It's toilsome and fruitless, frustratingly counterproductive, and difficult to align with God's purposes.

This is why so many people, including and sometimes especially Christians, assume work is bad. It's like it is bent in the wrong direction. But the origin story of work contradicts this assumption. Work was given as a good gift and an invitation to be cocreators with God.

When humanity rebelled against God and took work into their own hands, work got harder and less fruitful. *Yet work remains essential to life, and like everything else in God's created world, it needs redemption.*

This is why the second statement follows the first. Given that work is essential to life, make it good.

To redeem work or to work redemptively means, simply, turning bad and broken work into good and godly work wherever it is encountered. That is the task of the worker who follows Jesus.

If we as Christians see work the way God does, then we must find and seek to heal the brokenness in our daily work as people in the public, private, and social sectors. We must also find ways to make the work of family and the work of being a good neighbor redemptive.

Food is indeed essential to life. As we have seen, the same goes for all work, not just the business of food—from legal documents to car repairs, from government policy to fitness equipment, and from power line maintenance to wealth management. Renowned English essayist Dorothy L. Sayers clarifies the same point in her essay "Why Work?" when she says, "When a man or woman is called to a particular job of secular work, that is as true a vocation as though he or she were called to specifically religious work."[2]

Why? Because Christians can be more than just engaged, good, or successful workers. They can be redemptive workers. Every industry needs them to be.

Can you imagine Jesus turning a blind eye to bad systems, practices, and products in his industry of craftsmanship? Can you imagine Paul making inferior or mediocre products as a tentmaker? Jesus and Paul spent an awful lot of their time in everyday work, and I'm confident they found ways to work redemptively in their industries.

The daily work of Christians is the church's greatest opportunity to complement God's work. Yet for centuries, that opportunity has been largely ignored and often squandered. It must not continue.

What follows is a brief launching point for making your daily work redemptive that includes and goes beyond sharing your faith with a coworker, starting a workplace Bible study, or funding "spiritual" work, which are all good things. We will be challenged to think theologically about our industry and workplace, seek deep spiritual health personally, create good and beneficial work, embrace the relationships work brings, and serve others sacrificially.

Our hope is that this introduction to a rich theology of work would enliven your life and encourage you to bring meaning to your daily work in alignment with God's redemptive plan. When that happens, work in society will change, and people will see Jesus in a fresh, compelling way.

1

The Importance of Work

If we can accept [a] broader concept of mission as Christian service in the world comprising both evangelism and social action—a concept which is laid upon us by the model of our Saviour's mission in the world—then Christians could under God make a far greater impact on society.

JOHN STOTT

TODAY, MANY OF US are less than satisfied when it comes to our work lives. Beyond our jobs providing us with a paycheck, we don't really see any meaning or purpose in what we do day after day. We feel isolated from our colleagues at work, uncertain when it comes to understanding our calling, and conflicted when it comes to our personal faith and our public commitments in fields such as business, education, law, and health care. Finding answers to these dilemmas is essential if we want to live integrated, vital Christian lives—not just on Sundays but on the other six days too.

After all, we spend one-third of our adult lives at work, possibly more than ninety thousand hours. Life isn't all about work, but it's certainly a huge part of it. And if we don't approach our work with an understanding of *why* we do *what* we do—in a context that is greater than ourselves—our daily lives can easily feel disconnected from our faith. It's not intentional, of course, but our lack of coherence leads to us living in two separate and often disconnected worlds: church and work, private and public, values and facts.

There is no poverty worse than that which takes away work and the dignity of work. In a genuinely developed society, work is an essential dimension of social life, for it is not only a means of earning one's daily bread but also an avenue of personal growth, self-expression, the building of healthy relationships, and the exchange of gifts. Work gives us a sense of shared responsibility for the development of the world and, ultimately, for our life as a people.[1]

Was It Always Like This?

There was a time, according to the German sociologist Max Weber, when the world was like a "great enchanted garden"—when people understood the ordinary elements of their world and experience to be integrated into one great cosmic tapestry. Human work was thought to somehow participate in a greater, transcendent spiritual reality: there was no distinction between the sacred and the secular.

These days, most of us don't think about our work this way. According to Weber, starting with the Enlightenment of the eighteenth century, rapid modernization, a trend toward secularization, and the bureaucratization of work converged in what he called the "disenchantment of the world." No longer is the world viewed as an "enchanted garden" but instead as a barren, sterile environment where we feel alienated from one another and from the nature of our work.[2] As a result, for most of us in Western cultures, work has become thoroughly secular, divorced from any transcendent framework of ultimate meaning, stripped of any intrinsic value, and reduced to a means to an end—which is almost always the accumulation of material wealth. Faith is divorced from reason and forced out of the public square and into our private lives.

The net result has been a thoroughly dualistic worldview to which almost all modern Westerners subscribe without a second thought, many Christians included. Think of it this way: religious commitments have been confined to the private space and are considered inappropriate in the public square—such that if you were hosting a house party, you would expect to find guests in your living room but would be alarmed and offended to find them in your bedroom. Religious values, we might say, have been banished from the living room: what someone believes privately is their own business, so the thinking goes, but religious beliefs have no place in conversations of common concern. Thus Christianity went from being a public good to a private good, and now, in the minds of many, to a private ill.

For the Christian, an activity that is not sinful or displeasing to God is neither sacred nor secular in itself. But much Christian thinking is unwittingly shaped by dualistic assumptions, especially when it comes to work. For example, we may initially consider traditional ministry work—such as that of pastors, missionaries, or relief workers—to be more sacred than ordinary, secular work like practicing law, fitting pipes, or teaching eighth grade science. Indeed, dualism is still alive and well among Christians. According to a recent survey, 70 percent of American churchgoers don't see how their work serves God's purposes, and 78 percent see their work as less important than the work of a pastor or priest.[3]

This sacred/secular divide is a concept totally foreign to the New Testament, which teaches that all things done in and through Jesus Christ in the power of the Spirit are sacred.

We have gotten ourselves on the horns of a dilemma, true enough, but the dilemma is not real. It is a creature of misunderstanding. The sacred/secular antithesis has no foundation in the Old Testament or New Testament. Without doubt, a more perfect understanding of Christian truth will deliver us from it. As A. W. Tozer has written, "One of the greatest hindrances to internal peace which the Christian encounters is the common habit of dividing our lives into two areas—the sacred and the secular."[4]

We can turn to the Bible to dissolve this false sacred/secular divide and find a way to reintegrate faith and work:

- All things (including all industries and social systems) are being redeemed (Colossians 1:17-20).

- Sacred and secular are not just external realities but also include the public *and* private spheres (Luke 6:43-45).

- All activity can be done sacredly or secularly (Colossians 3:17, 23-24).

Doing our secular jobs in a spiritual way is a deeply Christian way of being in the world. As Lesslie Newbigin writes in his book *Truth to Tell*:

A serious commitment to evangelism, to the telling of the story which the Church is sent to tell, means a radical questioning of the reigning assumptions of public life. It is to affirm the gospel not only as an invitation to a private and personal decision but as public truth which ought to be acknowledged as true for the whole of the life of society.[5]

Making All Work Sacred

Work is our chance to participate in God's great plan to reconcile the world to himself in Christ. Work is our chance to participate in the redemption of all things. Work is where we shape our one small corner of the world. It doesn't matter if you are a lawyer, a factory worker, a plumber, a teacher, a stay-at-home parent, a full-time volunteer, a small business owner, or an entrepreneur, work is where you get the opportunity to form human civilization in all its specificity and beauty.

And let's be clear: when we talk about work, we are not talking only about paid positions or income-producing endeavors. The work of a stay-at-home parent who tirelessly cares for home and children is just as valuable as having a career in the corporate world. Work, whether paid or unpaid, is an opportunity for being involved spiritually in the world today.

As Christians, we have an amazing opportunity to engage with the culture during our normal, ordinary days. Faith and work should not be separate; instead, the heart of our faith is meant to be lived out during the day-to-day work of home and business.

In John Stott's classic little book *Christian Mission in the Modern World*, he asks a question that clarifies why the connection between our faith and our work is so important and relevant: *What exactly is the Christian mission? What has God sent the Church into the world to do?*

Knowing the answer to this question will help us to clearly answer two other important questions: What exactly are we as individuals sent to accomplish, and how does that relate to our work?[6] Jesus made it clear that his mission consisted of both words and deeds—and the Christian mission is meant to include both evangelistic and social responsibility. Therefore Stott concludes that work is at the heart of the Christian mission:

> Some are indeed called to be missionaries, evangelists or pastors, and others to the great professions of law, education, medicine and the social sciences. But others are called to commerce, to industry and farming, to accountancy and banking, to local government or parliament, and to the mass media. . . . In all these spheres, and many others besides, it is possible for Christians to interpret their lifework Christianly, and to see it . . . as their Christian vocation, as the way Christ has called them to spend their lives in his service.[7]

We can draw two major conclusions about the nature of work in light of Christian mission:

- Work is the greatest vehicle many of us have for loving our neighbors as ourselves. It's at work that we find our most frequent opportunities to serve the public good by using our talents and skills to serve others.

- Work is the context for disciplemaking and the verbal proclamation of the gospel of grace. Not all work activities will provide opportunities for sharing the good news, but most can be used by God to make us more Christ-like. And as God's Word shapes our motivation for our work, it will move out from our hearts to our mouths like a cup over-flowing with living water.

Let's look at the way these two conclusions provide solutions to two very important questions.

Question: How can we address the fact that the majority of the world doesn't know Christ, and knowledge of his truth is not found in the industries of our modern Western culture?

Solution: We can understand our work in light of the Christian faith. This involves learning and changing our thinking so we as Christians can witness to the gospel of grace and the universal lordship of Christ in a way that reaches those in our industry and culture.

Question: How can we help alleviate the suffering of a world filled with desperate social, environmental, spiritual, and cultural problems, ranging from jobs and justice to idols and empty hearts?

Solution: We can become servants of Christ through our daily work. We can learn to better serve others in our organizations, communities, and professions. As the body of Christ, we can help one another prepare for works of service in our daily work (see Ephesians 4:12).

Our hope is that this little book will increase the understanding of what it means for our faith to intersect with our work, and that through this understanding, our cities will be filled with disciples of Jesus—good citizens who will live out the implications of the gospel, not just in church on Sundays but every day in all of life. When our faith is integrated with our work, it transforms us to become passionate about finding the true, good, and beautiful in the work God has called us to do.

Our work is important because it represents God to the world. By adding our unique, creative input, we offer our work as a redemptive contribution to the culture and present our work in the world back to God as our gift to him.

2

The Real Story
of Work, in Short

There is a widespread notion in some of the most energetic contemporary Christian movements that the biblical call to reconciliation is solely about reconciling God and humanity, with no reference to social realities. In this view, preaching, teaching, church life and mission are only about a personal relationship between people and God. Christian energy is focused on winning converts, planting and growing churches, and evangelistic efforts.

EMMANUEL KATONGOLE AND CHRIS RICE

THE WAY WE THINK ABOUT WORK is tied to the way we think about the gospel. If our understanding of the gospel is too narrow, we will arrive at an *instrumental* understanding of our work, meaning that work is good only because of the value it can create for something else. But if we allow Scripture to expand our understanding, we can include an *intrinsic* view of our work, meaning work itself is valuable.

To illustrate, think of an instrumental and intrinsic view of human beings. If people are viewed primarily as instruments or tools, their intrinsic dignity is ignored or diminished. This is called dehumanization. An instrumental understanding of humanity leads to all kinds of atrocities like the Bernie Madoff Ponzi scheme, manipulating coworkers, and even the worst kind of human evil—genocide.

An instrumental view of work is not wrong, and it won't create evil on the same scale as dehumanization, but it is incomplete, and the effects are real. Work becomes the thing that leads to one's survival or success, sense of identity and status, or significance.

Seeing work through an intrinsic lens gives dignity to work, and with this broader understanding, we'll find ways to engage our work as part of God's mission to make all things new.

Too-Small Gospel Equals a Low View of Work

Many of us have grown up with a two-part gospel:

Part 1: Humans are sinners who are separated from God.

Part 2: Jesus died for our sins so that we can go to heaven to be with God when we die.

This is a powerful foundation, most certainly true, and absolutely good news. Yet there's more good news, and the rest is essential for how we understand work. The two-part gospel is not a helpful framework for thinking about the redemptive value of work because it's simply too narrow. How do our ordinary days fit into this understanding of the gospel? What are we supposed to be doing with our time here on earth while we wait to be with Jesus in heaven? This truncated gospel usually coincides with an *instrumental* view of work: we work so we can earn money to give it away to churches and nonprofits that are doing the "real" work of Christian mission.

But the gospel is more than these two parts. It is a drama that unfolds from beginning to end and across Scripture in four acts—creation, fall, redemption, and new creation. This expanded view helps us to see how our work fits into God's grand mission to reconcile to himself *all things* (not just individual sinners) in heaven and earth (Ephesians 1:10; Colossians 1:20). The good news of the four-part gospel is much better than we realize, and it also means the bad news is much worse than we might have thought. Here's what we mean:

1. ***Creation:*** The creation accounts in Genesis depict a good and wise Creator who shows himself to be collaborative in nature, meaning he "works with." He freely shares himself and his work with the only creatures who bear his image: human beings (see Genesis 1:28-31; 2:15-25). Very significantly, we see that work *predates* the fall into sin and death, and we realize that work is one of the original goods of creation. The fundamental goodness of work shows up most explicitly in what is often referred to as the *cultural mandate*, as God commissions human beings to care for creation and make it flourish (see Genesis 1:28-30 and 2:15). In this regard, to be a human being is to be a creature who has tasks to do—we are drawn into

God's dynamic work of creation and asked to care for what he has made. We are responsible to God for the work we do.

2. **Fall:** The event known as the fall—a cataclysmic rebellion against God that plunged the entire created order into a state of disarray and bondage (see Genesis 3–11; Romans 8:19-23)—disrupted the harmoniousness of God's good creation on multiple levels. The fall and its implications are both *personal* and *cosmic* in scope, tainting what we call the Five Key Relationships:

   - Our relationship to our true selves (psychological)

   - Our relationship with one another (social)

   - Our relationship to systems and structures (systemic)

   - Our relationship to the created order (ecological)

   - Our relationship to God (theological)

Because of the fall, we do our daily work as both *fallen* and *falling*, and we seek to fulfill the cultural mandate within systems, industries, economies, cities, states, and nations that have all been twisted and warped by sin.

3. **_Redemption_:** All human life—including all
human work—exists in the shadow of the fall. God
intervenes repeatedly from Genesis 3 throughout
the Old Testament. He rescues and forms a people
to become a priestly nation with guidance for life
and work for all the nations (Genesis 12:1-3; Exodus
19:5-6). Then, as the New Testament tells it, God
has taken radical and decisive action through the
life, death, resurrection, and ascension of Jesus
Christ to "reconcile to himself all things, whether
on earth or in heaven" (Colossians 1:20 NRSV).
Just as the fall is both personal and cosmic, so the
cure is both personal and cosmic, and once we recognize this, we'll discover new purpose for our
work. With a broader vision of redemption in mind,
our work is no longer an instrumental means to an
end, but in a limited sense it's actually an end in
itself. Our work is not salvific—that is, it is not the
answer to the curse that haunts creation—but because of Jesus, it is one of the ways that God invites
his people to join in his mission to bring heaven and
earth together in Christ (Ephesians 1:10).

4. ***New creation:*** It is central to the Bible's main storyline that God intends to redeem and restore his fallen creation, not abandon it. Contrary to some popular misunderstandings of the end times, Jesus Christ is not rescuing us *from* the world; he is rescuing us *for the life of the world.* Revelation 21–22 depicts a new heaven and a new earth, which God has finally reintegrated in a perfect city, including the very systems and structures that have been pulled apart and twisted by sin and death. And it gets better: the New Testament makes the bold claim that it is possible for God's people, by the power of the Holy Spirit, to live in such a way that not only *anticipates* God's future reign when all things will be made new, but to live in such a way that *participates* in this future, which Christians call the kingdom of God. Our challenge is to imagine how our work can serve as a sign and a foretaste of the kingdom of God that is both here already and will come fully as a perfect city.

This four-part gospel provides a complete framework for our life here on earth. It helps us understand that we are meant to participate in God's grand mission of redemption by living life *with* God for the life of the world *through* our work. God does his work of reconciling all things, all five of the key relationships, to himself through *our* work!

The Full Story and Why It Matters

For the gospel to be orthodox—meaning historically affirmed and true—it must include individuals being saved by grace through faith in Christ. But to be orthodox, it also must include more than the redemption of individual souls. We're reminded that God is "pleased to reconcile to himself all things" (Colossians 1:20 NRSV). And "all things" there involves a very technical Greek phrase that means . . . well . . . "all things."

Redemption work happens biblically in alignment with the five key relationships we highlighted above. God wants our work to join his work to address the brokenness in our world in these ways:

1. ***Redemption with God***—salvation, making possible our union and communion with Christ both now and eternally. This means living as an

example and picture of Christ at work and sharing his good news appropriately and thoughtfully in the context of our working relationships.

2. ***Redemption in our lives***—sanctification, or the healing and transformation of our thoughts, words, and deeds for God's purposes. This includes our motivations and attitudes, our workplace performance anxiety, the idols of our hearts, and even how we influence and lead others.

3. ***Redemption with one another***—seeking forgiveness, making peace, loving our enemies, or not repaying a coworker's attempts to malign us or otherwise hurt us.

4. ***Redemption of systems and structures***—transforming the way the fall has affected systems, processes, policies, methods, and procedures. Today this could relate to compensation practices, policies affecting or even causing a city's affordable housing crisis, harmful payday lending practices, human trafficking, implicit bias in hiring, or multitiered health care rules for different employees within the same organization.

5. ***Redemption of the created world***—making new every aspect of creation groaning to be "liberated from its bondage to decay" (Romans 8:21). This could include our concern for the misuse and abuse of natural resources, the pollution of our oceans, and the neglect of our forest lands creating unnecessary wildfires.

As we sing triumphantly each Christmas in the classic carol "Joy to the World," "He comes to make his blessings flow, far as the curse is found." What a gorgeous vision! Does the work of Christ on the cross apply chiefly to restoring individuals to union with himself? Yes. *And* it must extend beyond that to all the ways God is healing sin's corrupting effects on the flourishing of humanity and creation. As God's people, we partner with him in his redemption and restoration of all things through our daily work.

Why does this matter? People frequently say they don't see the spiritual significance of their "secular" jobs. At best, they've been taught an *instrumental view* of the sacredness of work—it's a means to earn money and give to God's mission, and it allows us to build relationships to share the gospel.

As we have seen, the answer is, "Well, yes, but also no."

Work includes, but is way more than, an instrument or platform for the mission of an individual's salvation. A fuller, broadened biblical framework for redemption allows us to see our story and work in the world as more deeply rooted in God's story and his work in the world.

Do you see how a more intrinsic view of work can transform your daily occupation into something redemptive, something that brings God's reconciling purposes to fruition where you live and work?

3

Created and Placed
by God for Good Work

Work for the peace and prosperity

of the city where I sent you.

JEREMIAH 29:7 NLT

WORK IS THE GREATEST OPPORTUNITY many of us have for fulfilling the calling of Christ and his command to love our neighbors as ourselves. Reflect on that statement. What if every Christ-follower really believed that? Building sewage systems, creating businesses, teaching graduate students, caring for the elderly, establishing order through the legal system, picking up toys on the living room floor—this is neighborly love and a key component of God's mission to redeem and restore all things.

It is at work where we often see our greatest opportunities to use our talents and skills to love and serve others. It is at work where we can make the richness of God's wisdom known to all. Therefore, we must allow God's Word to shape our minds, hearts, and motivations for our work, and his Spirit will produce much fruit.

Created in God's Image

To understand work in God's plan, we need to go back to the beginning once again, back to the basics of what it means to be a human being. We are created to bear God's image, often referred to using the Latin words *imago Dei*.

> Then God said, "Let us make human beings in our image, to be like us." . . .
>
> So God created human beings in his own image.
>   In the image of God he created them;
>   male and female he created them.
>   (Genesis 1:26-27 NLT)

But what does it really mean to be made in God's image?

It means human beings have been created by God with the unique ability to reason and communicate in complex languages, the capacity to exercise free will and a moral sense, and the ability to relate to one another. We were also given instructions to work alongside God in the care and cultivation of the earth. Our work is to help creation flourish by cultivating (developing resources) and caring for it as we read in Genesis 2:15: "Then the LORD God took the man and put him in the Garden of Eden to cultivate it and tend it" (NASB).

Created for Good Work

Each of us today has been given the gift of specific work to do that is intended to align with the cultural mandate of Genesis 1:28, as Paul tells us in Ephesians 2:10: "We are God's masterpiece. He has created us anew in Christ Jesus, so we can do the good things he planned for us long ago" (NLT).

As creations especially precious to God, we have the privilege to be colaborers with God in his great plan to reconcile the world to himself in Christ. Paid and unpaid work allows us to participate in God's redemption and restoration of all things, and that is where God has placed us to shape our small corners of the world. It doesn't matter if you work for pay or volunteer. Work is where you get the opportunity to form and to cultivate human civilization in all its God-given specificity and beauty.

As Christians today, we have an amazing mission to engage with the culture during our normal, ordinary days at work as an act of worship. The heart of our faith is meant to be lived out during the day-to-day work in every aspect of our economy and society. This is what it means to be a person made in the image of God, created to do the good works he has prepared for us to do long ago.

Created for a Place

We've been made in God's image and created for work. We were also made for a place—the original one was the Garden of Eden. In this location, God's image bearers worked alongside him to care for and cultivate the garden. All five key relationships were right and in order, but it didn't last.

We all hunger for a sense of place, a sense of belonging. But because of the fall, our relationship to the physical spaces where we live, love, and work is fundamentally broken. All of us as human beings exist within a *crisis of place*.

It started in Genesis with Adam. His name means "soil creature" or "earthling" and comes from the Hebrew *adamah*, which translates as "soil" or "cultivatable ground." In the beginning, God meant his newly created human beings to have an organic relationship with their place in the world. However as we read in Genesis 3:23-24, because of Adam and Eve's sin, human beings were separated from their place and have since existed in a state of displacement. In a final and painful result of the curse, human beings are still charged with caring for the earth, but now they will be forced to do it as exiles.

Helmut Thielicke, in his book *Being Human . . . Becoming Human*, suggests that this fundamental alienation still characterizes our human existence. The suffering experienced in being displaced is not just reserved for refugees or those who have been exiled. We are all exiles looking for our true place of belonging, our true home. Even though we are displaced, Thielicke says, "home and place are part of human identity. We have our being in that which sustains us in the history that we live, in the houses in which we dwell." He goes on to say that "losing all these, we lose ourselves."[1]

We are people who live out our physical histories in tangible places that shape and form us. But like every other aspect of our existence, our relationship to place has been warped by sin and is in need of redemption.

The entire Bible can be read as a "theology of place": God's saving action to redeem this crisis of place and bring human beings back home. If we look for this theme, we can see it again and again in the biblical storyline.

- God promises to bring about the blessing of all people through the family of Abraham and a *place* is at the center of his plan. In time this place, the land of Canaan, will become a new Eden, where all the peoples of the earth will dwell in peace and security (see Genesis 17).

- The prophet Isaiah dreams of a future where God dwells together with humans in a *place* where the curses of Genesis 3 are totally reversed. In a striking image, Isaiah says that this will be the "most important place on earth," and on that day humans will "hammer their swords into plowshares and their spears into pruning hooks" (Isaiah 2:2, 4 NLT).

- The biblical story reaches its culmination in the book of Revelation, where, next to God, a *place* is the main character. The apostle John describes a beautiful city prepared by God himself. The displaced exiles who have been wandering "east of Eden" with only a faint hope that they will ever be able to dwell in peace and security will finally come home at last (see Revelation 21–22). It's the new Jerusalem, the new city of shalom, a place where all five of the key relationships are fully restored.

Today, as faithful stewards of the work God has entrusted to us, we can begin to address this crisis of place by identifying the specific forms of placelessness we see around us in our workplaces and where we live. For instance, as we look around our urban neighborhoods, we see buildings with ample private space but very little public space. In our inner cities, the trend toward gentrification is literally displacing residents, and homelessness, too, is a massive problem of displacement.

Another form of placelessness can be seen in business, where outsourcing often means work is being done by people who do not live in the communities they serve.

Large corporations can sometimes be impersonal, lacking local character or presence. Technology, too, has contributed to this sense of being displaced as remote work continues becoming a norm. More and more business is conducted in "the cloud"—which is not an actual place at all. Zoom has replaced gathering together in conference rooms to meet and interact. Social media normalizes disincarnate relationships that do not exist in concrete spaces. The pandemic, of course, added to all these trends.

Do Good Work in the Place Where God Placed You

God, however, intends us to flourish where we are, in the places where we live and work, in our communities. Perhaps one of the best examples of this is Jeremiah 29:5-7 (NLT), where God instructs the Israelites who have been exiled from their homes in Jerusalem and sent to Babylon as follows:

> Build homes, and plan to stay. Plant gardens, and eat the food they produce. Marry and have children. Then find spouses for them so that you may have many grandchildren. Multiply! Do not dwindle away! And work for the peace and prosperity of the

city where I sent you into exile. Pray to the LORD for
it, for its welfare will determine your welfare.

The good work God called the exiles of Israel to do
was not evangelism. It was the daily grind of working:
building, planting, harvesting, raising children, getting
and staying married. This work was essential for living,
for increasing in a particular place that was not their final
home. They longed for Jerusalem.

Similarly, Christ's followers today are in exile no matter
where they live—whether a nation, city, street, or workplace. And we all long for new Jerusalem. But because of
Christ, we can make the essential work of daily living
good by bringing a sign and foretaste of heaven, that final
city, to earth where God placed us.

This crisis of place can feel overwhelming, but as followers of Jesus we are not to be passive but rather people
filled with hope. As we "work for the peace and prosperity" of the cities where we live, serving others selflessly,
we can embody this theology of place and be part of
God's transforming solution.

4

The Reality of Work and Calling

"The priesthood of all believers" did not make everyone into church workers; rather, it turned every kind of work into a sacred calling.

GENE EDWARD VEITH, *GOD AT WORK*

SIN HAS DEEPLY WOUNDED OUR WORLD more than we typically recognize. The fall, with its descent into decay and corruption, affected not only human beings but also the systems and structures of our world. That's why so many of us experience disappointment, failure, or even deep pain in our work. Instead of being meaningful, as God intended, work itself has been twisted and distorted, often feeling meaningless and futile. Even with all our scientific and technological advances, brokenness continues to invade our work and crops up again and again.

Work itself has been corrupted in several ways:

- ***Our work appears fruitless.*** We don't seem to be able to accomplish what we think we're meant to do with our lives.

- ***Our work doesn't materialize as we hope it will.*** No matter how hard we try, we feel stalled or run into roadblock after roadblock.

- ***Our work feels pointless.*** We become alienated from our work and lose sight of its purpose. Whether we're staring at our computers, waiting tables, or driving a delivery truck, we have no idea whether what we're doing makes any difference.

- ***Our work consumes us.*** We are consumed by work in an unhealthy way; we develop an unholy appetite for achievement and recognition, even at the expense of our most important relationships.

- ***Our work is our idol.*** We make a god out of our accomplishments and slowly (and usually unwittingly) become conformed to the distorted image of what we worship. Before we know it, we've confused our job with our identity. Our work becomes the story of our own personal success and a means to serve ourselves rather than the vehicle by which we serve God, our neighbors, and society.

This paints a rather grim picture, with our work falling somewhere between the extremes of futility on one end and idolatry on the other. But this is not how God intended work to be, nor is it the way the Bible portrays the purpose of work, despite the way sin threatens our efforts through futility and frustration.

The Bible describes work as the way we can live into a new story, one that shows how the good news of the gospel through the work of Jesus Christ equips us with courage, diligence, and the hopefulness that make all things new. Though we will continue to feel and experience the effect of humanity's continuing rebellion against God in our work, the four-part gospel (see chapter two) provides new and hope-filled ways of thinking about how our daily work can be part of God's redemptive mission in the world. Our work can be the channel for confronting and ultimately overcoming the fruitlessness, pointlessness, selfishness, and idolatry that plague today's work culture this side of paradise.

When we begin to see work—our occupation and responsibilities—as an invitation to participate in God's reconciliation of all that is broken, we start to infuse our daily tasks with a sense of purpose and calling.

When Work Meets Brokenness, We Find a Calling

What is my calling? is a common question these days. We talk a lot about work being an expression of our God-given identity, and this creates a sense that work should be purposeful and intentional. People want to know that what they're doing matters to God, that they're doing what God wants them to do.

Many people—Christian or not—have adopted the word *calling* or *vocation* as a way to instill their daily work with meaning and purpose. But in today's world, the concept of *vocation* often takes on all kinds of cultural assumptions that more or less equate *vocation* with "occupation."

The etymology of *vocation* comes from the Latin words *vox* ("voice"), *vocare* ("to call"), and *vocatio* ("a summons").

Thus, the idea of vocation is embedded in variations of *calling*. Simply, this means *vocation* and *calling* are largely synonymous. This leads us to the conclusion that the concept of vocation is much bigger and more significant than a particular job.

In the Christian worldview, the concept of *calling* acknowledges that each human being has been addressed by someone beyond themself and tasked with a particular responsibility in the world. In the Bible, God routinely calls people into a relationship with himself. Here *calling* is used in a few different ways. It can refer to the responsibility we all have as bearers of God's image, or it can mean God's universal call to salvation, issued to all people in every time and place. More narrowly, it can refer to instances in which God singles out individuals for a unique task or purpose, such as the call of Abram (see Genesis 12) or the commissioning of the first disciples (see Mark 1:16-20). But in every case, biblical calling refers to God's summons to a person—or to a people—with an expectation of a response.

In his book *The Call*, Os Guinness distinguishes between primary calling and secondary calling.[1] Every believer has a primary calling as a person belonging to

God. As believers, we have a calling to live out a lifestyle befitting of a certain kind of identity—namely, as those sanctified ("set apart") for God's purposes and presence. So our primary calling is to "walk in a manner worthy of the calling with which [we] have been called" (Ephesians 4:1 NASB). Believers are called to this identity *before* they are called to any specific professional capacity.

Calling is foundationally relational; God calls us into union and communion with Christ. This is our primary calling, and it applies to every area of our lives, including our work and occupation. We can't forget that God is primarily calling us to himself.

Our secondary calling is unique to each of us. This involves a process of discernment, and discernment takes time. It's not always easy to translate biblical principles into the marketplace. For instance, we talk about trusting God with our work. How does that inform how we choose a college major? How do we trust God as we sort through job postings online? How do we translate biblical principles into actually building a career? How can we realistically combine timeless spiritual truths with real-world application?

Discerning and understanding our specific individual calling is about holding these things in our hands as worship to God and as service to the world. This secondary calling will look different for each one of us because we're unique and different. And the questions being answered here are more about, Who am I, How am I supposed to live, and Why am I supposed to live?

Many times we equate our job with our calling, our current occupation with our vocation, and we are encouraged to "do a job that you love." But this is misguided at best; not everyone has the personal agency and resources to make such a choice. Ultimately, "do what you love" can devolve into a self-focused illusion of seeking a job that may never exist. A biblical understanding of calling provides a much deeper satisfaction of following God in every circumstance, in every place, no matter our like or dislike of a particular job.

Spiritual Practices for Discerning One's Calling

So how can you approach your calling to include work? What difference does it make in your work life when you do? Here are three spiritual disciplines that can help us discern a sense of calling—always keeping in mind that spiritual practices help set the tone, but they don't make our decisions for us.

Seek solitude in silence. This is being still and knowing that God is God (see Psalm 46). It involves freeing yourself from the noise in your environment . . . and also from the noise in your own mind. This is similar to mindfulness and meditation—which are so popular today—but for Christians, the goal is not to empty the self but rather to create space for focused attention on God.

Practice reading Scripture deeply. This means reading the Bible for more than information; it's more the experience of placing yourself within the text and thinking deeply about how your own identity shows up in light of God's work of redemption. It can be described as a careful, meditative reading in which you dwell on words and phrases that speak to you in a unique way.

Pray with quiet trust. Here you acknowledge your complete dependence on God and surrender to him. You ask God to help you surrender to his will, and you become indifferent to anything other than his will. You seek to gain wisdom in making decisions about your life.

When we have a sense of both our primary and secondary calling, we move away from seeing our vocation as needing to be the ultimate personal choice of a career or a particular job, and we see it more about exploring every opportunity put before us, including work, to love God and love our neighbor well.

5

Work in a Politicized and Polarized Society

For you are all children of the light and of the day; we don't belong to darkness and night. So be on your guard, not asleep like the others. Stay alert and be clearheaded.

1 THESSALONIANS 5:5-6 NLT

WHAT DOES IT LOOK LIKE FOR CHRISTIANS to engage their culture faithfully and redemptively in their daily work? This is a complicated question. Our current political and cultural climate is already deeply divided and becoming more polarized all the time; the nature of the public square itself is changing from physical to virtual, and cultural norms are changing dramatically.

Pluralism is on the rise, and fewer and fewer of our neighbors identify as "religious" in the traditional sense. Some Christians are tempted to respond to all this with fear and cynicism, while many others retreat into passivity, keeping silent and doing nothing about current issues.

We can no longer assume that our culture is Christian, even in a nominal sense. Recent demographic research demonstrates that American culture is becoming more and more secularized. For instance, a significant number of respondents held a negative view of Christianity's role in society, and an overwhelming majority characterized Christians as judgmental. A 2007 Barna report stated, "Among young non-Christians, nine out of the top 12 perceptions were negative. Common negative perceptions include that present-day Christianity is judgmental (87%), hypocritical (85%), old-fashioned (78%), and too involved in politics (75%)."[1]

Yet our faith calls us not away from the world but toward it. How do we actively engage in our common life with fellow citizens and neighbors who may not share our beliefs or values?

According to the apostle Paul, Christians have been entrusted with the "message of reconciliation," commissioned to bring peace where there is discord and to resolve conflicts wherever they are found. "So we are Christ's ambassadors," he says, "God is making his appeal through us. We speak for Christ when we plead, 'Come back to God!'" (2 Corinthians 5:19-20 NLT).

It's no mistake that Paul refers to believers as holding the political office of ambassador. And to serve as effective diplomats on Christ's behalf, what we need is not necessarily a particular set of policies (although Christians will have their convictions) but the *wisdom* to negotiate complex questions in the public square and the *virtues* of courage, humility, and respect to live our common life faithfully.

Our challenge as Christians is to cultivate faithful work practices such as:

- celebrating the good and reforming the broken

- maintaining a distinct Christian mentality and manner of life

- seeking what is best for our neighbors—coworkers, clients, bosses, vendors, and customers

- finding common ground
- being winsome and unapologetic regarding our convictions and motivations while respecting the convictions and motivations of others
- creatively exceeding and surprising the culture's expectations of what a Christian is

As citizens, we are called to participate in the political process, but it's not only through our vote that we influence the public square. It's also through believing, declaring, and embodying the gospel in our daily lives as we join with our nonbelieving neighbors in the struggle against injustice and brokenness in our workplaces and communities.

Straddling Two Ages

For the writers of the New Testament, the Christian life is lived at the intersection of two ages—the present age, which is ruled by sin and darkness, and the age to come, which has been inaugurated in the life, death, and resurrection of Jesus Christ.[2] It's not uncommon for these authors to characterize the former age as darkness and the coming age as light, as Paul does in

1 Thessalonians 5:5-6: "You are all children of the light and of the day; we don't belong to darkness and night. So be on your guard, not asleep like the others. Stay alert and be clearheaded" (NLT).

The trouble is, Christians are tasked with living as daytime people even as the darkness of night still lingers over every human endeavor. It simply is in the nature of human existence to be constrained by impossible situations where it is difficult to discern what is right and true, and it's even more difficult to act on those judgments. To translate the predicament into our concrete American context, during an election, no matter whom we vote for, we'll be endorsing some of our values but betraying others; every policy solves one problem but creates another.

So, where does this leave us? On one level, it sounds like a recipe for despair. If every human effort is tainted by sin and self-interest, and if every politician has an agenda, and if every party platform is morally dubious, and if all human accomplishments are only partial at best, should Christians just withdraw from the political process altogether, try to be decent people, and get along as best we can?

Christian Realism

Reinhold Niebuhr took a different approach, which has been characterized as *Christian realism*—*Christian* in that it affirms the real potential for redemption of unjust systems and structures in history, and *realism* in that it is unflinching about the power of self-interest to warp and twist even our most moral actions. Faithful Christian engagement doesn't necessarily require a particular set of policy positions but rather the *wisdom and courage to live responsibly* in an ambiguous world. We need to be proactive and discover where God is already at work making all things new: "The final victory over man's disorder is God's and not ours; but we do have responsibility for proximate victories," wrote Niebuhr in 1953. "We can neither renounce this early home of ours nor yet claim that its victories and defeats give the final meaning to our existence."[3]

On this point Niebuhr sounds an awful lot like the apostle Peter. And that's by design: Christian realism is an attempt to recover the unique political theology of the New Testament. Here's how the apostle Peter puts it:

> For the Lord's sake, submit to all human authority—
> whether the king as head of state, or the officials he

has appointed. For the king has sent them to punish those who do wrong and to honor those who do right.

It is God's will that your honorable lives should silence those ignorant people who make foolish accusations against you. For you are free, yet you are God's slaves, so don't use your freedom as an excuse to do evil. Respect everyone, and love the family of believers. Fear God, and respect the king. (1 Peter 2:13-17 NLT)

Peter's primary concern is to put politics into its proper place by reminding the saints where their ultimate allegiances should lie. The key to the passage comes at the very end: "Fear God, and respect the king." These six words are the germ of a thoughtful political theology for our cultural moment. In these six words, Peter captures something critical about what politics is and what it is not, and about what politics demands of us and what it does not.

In our age of ideology, Peter's words should sting a little. If we really are "temporary residents" on this earth (1 Peter 2:11 NLT), then we *should feel a little out of place*, as though our values don't quite line up with those of our host society. If we find that everything we believe perfectly aligns with one political platform or the other, we might ask ourselves if our ideology is driving our theology, or if, as it should be, our theology is driving our ideology. If we get this wrong, maybe we've forgotten where our homeland really is.

Political engagement in general—but especially Christian political engagement—is not clean-cut. It's not a matter of just checking a box or getting your vote to line up on one certain side of the aisle. It's wrestling with tough issues and realizing that chances are no politician, no candidate, no party is a perfect reflection of the Christian faith.

Yet in the end we must deal with the world as it is, not as we wish it were. Although we are temporary residents, we are residents nonetheless. "So be careful how you live. Don't live like fools, but like those who are wise. Make the most of every opportunity in these evil days" (Ephesians 5:15-16 NLT).

There are no easy solutions. But as you think deeply about your role as a Christian citizen in the twenty-first century, you'll gain deeper wisdom for the tough days ahead as well as new ways to effectively live out Christ's command to love God and love your neighbors.

6

Monday Through Saturday Missionaries

So, my dear brothers and sisters, be strong and immovable. Always work enthusiastically for the Lord, for you know that nothing you do for the Lord is ever useless.

1 CORINTHIANS 15:58 NLT

EVERY SUNDAY, WE ARE SENT BACK OUT into the world for another week. But just what is the church sent out into the world to do?[1]

It's a fundamental question. We know that our motivation for ministry is the gospel of Jesus Christ, his atoning death for our sins, and his resurrection for our salvation. The free gift of new life in Christ is the spark that ignites the heart of his global people.

But what are we, the church, to actually *do* about it? John Stott, the framer of the Lausanne Covenant, pastor of All Souls Church in London for half a century, and bestselling author, saw a unity between service and witness; he saw them both as being central to the church's mission. Both are at the heart of why God sent Jesus himself into the world.

The authors of *The Missional Church* agree. "The church's own mission," they write, "must take its cues from the way God's mission unfolded in the sending of Jesus into the world for its salvation." They also identify a three-part structure to the church's own mission: "In Jesus' way of carrying out God's mission, we discover that the church is to represent God's reign as its community, its servant, and its messenger."[2]

In other words, the church is sent:

1. To live under the reign of God as a distinctive covenant community

2. To represent the reign of God by its actions and to serve the world with the passion of God

3. To proclaim the good news of Jesus Christ, inviting everyone to enter the kingdom by way of the atoning sacrifice of Christ

What if our daily work is what we, as the church, are sent out each Sunday to do? What if our daily work is the central place where the church—Monday through Saturday—embodies the gospel in daily living, bears witness to the truth of Christ in all of life, and serves the needs of the world?

What would change if the daily work of men and women was the center point of how all churches understand their own mission to their community rather than church-led initiatives carried out by volunteers? How would this change the church's preaching, teaching, and programming?

Elton Trueblood, the great twentieth-century theologian, said in his little-known book *The Common Ventures of Life*, "A Church which seeks to lift our sagging civilization will preach the principle of vocation in season and out of season. The message is that the world is one, secular and sacred, and that the chief way to serve the Lord is in our daily work."[3]

And missionary, apologist, and theologian Lesslie Newbigin said something similar:

> We need to create, above all, possibilities in every congregation for laypeople to share with one another the actual experience of their weekday work and to seek illumination from the gospel for their daily secular duty. Only thus shall we begin to bring together what our culture has divided—the public and the private. Only thus will the church fulfill its proper missionary role.[4]

In our modern Western culture, which has become a pluralistic society ruled in the public realm by a secular view of the world, work is the context in which the church bears witness to Christ as Lord over all of life. The only alternative is to retreat into the private sphere without a word of hope for the public life of the world.

But in so many churches, we hear about lots of ministries involving kids, teens, young marrieds, men, women, and singles. There is no shortage of "mission activities," which in most cases means volunteering. *But where is work?*

Where are the efforts to bear witness to Christ and make his present and coming kingdom visible in corporate boardrooms, public schools, or hospitals? Where is the equipping of the saints for deep acts of love and service in the manual trades, manufacturing, the service industry, or accounting? Aren't all these opportunities for serving too? Isn't this where all of us listening to weekly sermons spend our weeks—and our lives?

Let's not stop volunteering. We *need* volunteers; we *need* nonprofits. Society crumbles without those stepping in the gap to care for the poor on a volunteer basis. But isn't job creation in business central to economic development too? Protecting and serving those in need are dependent on how we do our work, whether it be that of a police officer, lawyer, or entrepreneur.

To make a real difference in our present culture, we need, as Robert Bellah suggests in his book *Habits of the Heart*, to recover "the idea of work as a contribution to the good of all and not merely as a means to one's own advancement."[5] This means that our day-to-day tasks, no matter how small, when done as a response to God's calling, matter from an eternal perspective. This is the promise of our Christian faith.

English crime novelist, poet, and playwright Dorothy L. Sayers thought deeply about the subject of work and vocation. "Work," she said, "is not, primarily, a thing one does to live, but the thing one lives to do." She went on to say that work "should be the full expression of the worker's faculties, the thing in which he finds spiritual, mental, and bodily satisfaction, and the medium in which he offers himself to God."[6]

Sayers believed that our whole attitude toward work needed a "thoroughgoing revolution":

It should be looked upon—not as a necessary drudgery to be undergone for the purpose of making money, but as a way of life in which the nature of man should find its proper exercise and delight and so fulfill itself to the glory of God. That it should, in fact, be thought of as a creative activity undertaken for the love of the work itself; and that man, made in God's image, should make things, as God makes them, for the sake of doing well a thing that is well worth doing.[7]

The challenge for the church in the twenty-first century will be whether our vision of mission includes the world of work or overlooks it in its preaching, teaching, and programming.

This is the challenge for the church in a post-Christian society. And this is the call of the heart of God, who has sent his covenant community into the world to faithfully live, witness, and serve.

7

Rest for and in the Working

For centuries we have preached to the hurrying people: your daily rush has no meaning, yet accept it—and you will be rewarded in another world by an eternal rest. But God revealed and offers us eternal Life and not eternal rest. And God revealed this eternal Life in the midst of time—and of its rush—as its secret meaning and goal.

ALEXANDER SCHMEMANN,
FOR THE LIFE OF THE WORLD

AS WE COME TO THE FINAL CHAPTER, we hope to have stirred your mind and heart toward a renewed vision of daily work. Work is not only an important area of life to live with faithfulness to Christ, it is also central to his redemptive work in the world. It's not something we can compartmentalize, and it's not something we can relegate to the sidelines of ministry.

In a society rampant with anxiety, this chapter hopes to give you a renewed vision of rest. The elusive pursuit of work-life balance is a constant point of tension in individual career choices and between employers and employees. In search of the perfect balance, employers increasingly offer support in terms of more flexible schedules, remote work options, fitness and nutrition benefits, childcare considerations, and mental health resources. These efforts should be commended as they are especially helpful for marginalized workers.[1] Their increase points to a sense that workers need support from work in order to develop a healthy life. They also point out that work is a master we have to work around to feel rested.

A renewed vision for rest is a necessary complement to a renewed vision for work. But adding our work lives to the list of things Christ makes demands on could sound exhausting, perhaps even defeating. It may not feel like rest. However, it is not surprising that Jesus has a bigger, restored vision for our work. His new vision for work includes a vision for rest too.

We need to reconsider how God's design of work and rest sustains and restores us in our work and in our whole lives.

Jesus extends to us an invitation to rest: "Come to me, . . . and I will give you rest." His yoke is easy and his burden is light (Matthew 11:28-30). In other words, he's not the kind of boss that punishes employees who depend on his provision when they do not meet the demands of the job. He's not the kind of boss that makes impossible demands and provides little resources for accomplishing them.

No, he has extended an invitation for humanity to join him in his creative and redemptive work. It is work that *he* will complete; he does not depend on us to complete it. We depend on him. This truth gives us freedom. As pastor Timothy Keller and Katherine Leary Alsdorf put it in their book *Every Good Endeavor*, Christians have "an identity and significance untethered to their job or financial status. They [are] no longer controlled by their work."[2]

Coming to live in this reality means understanding and living in the rest God offers. Rest in Christ is our primary, most central reality. There is no striving to prove worthiness or value, no scraping by to sustain a lifestyle, no saving ourselves from despair, and no sense of working to feel fulfilled in and of ourselves. Rest in Christ is true freedom—freedom from a yoke that is hard and a burden that is heavy.

Rest as a Practice

Scripture's view of work and rest is founded on the idea of Sabbath. While Sabbath may not be a popular idea in current culture, understanding Sabbath is crucial to grasp why and how we find rest *in* work and *from* work. At the end of Genesis 1 and the beginning of Genesis 2, God's rest from his work is emphatically emphasized.

God saw all that he had made, and it was very good. And there was evening, and there was morning— the sixth day. (Genesis 1:31)

The heavens and the earth were completed in all their vast array. By the seventh day God had finished the work he had been doing; so on the seventh day he rested from all his work. Then God blessed the seventh day and made it holy, because on it he rested from all the work of creating that he had done. (Genesis 2:1-3)

The text is repetitive and insistent to the reader: God finished his work, and then he rested. The *Theology of Work Commentary* says, "The polarity that actually undergirds the Sabbath is *work* and *rest*."[3] When Moses gives the Ten Commandments in Exodus, the fourth one is patterned after this refrain in Genesis. Typically, Christians today think of the Sabbath command as ensuring one day of the week is set aside for rest. But as the *Theology of Work Commentary* points out, "Both work and rest are included in the fourth commandment. The six days of work are as much a part of the commandment as the one day of rest."[4]

The rest God patterns for humanity and then commands Israel to practice first requires work that is good and fruitful. It is a command to work and to rest. The fruitful work is cause for delight, which is celebrated and acknowledged on the seventh day. God's rest from and delight in his work go together. As Christians, practicing the Sabbath, then, is not merely a break from work. It's actively enjoying and delighting in the *fruit* of the work given by God for us to do (Ephesians 2:10) that we have completed in service to him and to others.

Real rest is tied directly to our self-understanding as being in Christ and working toward his purposes. In neither work nor rest, in neither workaholism and overwork, nor leisure and self-amusement, should we hope to find who we are and what our purpose is. Today's ideas of rest "may lead less to the fulfilling and joyful rest we were made for and more toward the sin of acedia [not caring]," which in turn, "opens you to letting all the other sins be the motivations for your work. It puts the cynical self at the center of your life."[5]

Working too much and not working at all or without real care are what happens when we fail to live in accordance with the pattern of work and rest God intended for us. Andy Crouch shows the real value of the Sabbath for work and rest when he says, "Just as the cessation of work is an incentive to make the work on our other days more focused and faithful, the promise of sabbath's weekly festivity—not some distant holiday or vacation, but every seventh day—reorients us toward the truth about God and God's very good world."[6]

God's intention for work and rest is not a work-life balance approach. Work-life balance sets work and life in opposition to one another, with limitations to work getting all the attention. It is as if work is the necessary evil that strips us of our individual freedom. The reaction to the workplace's ever-increasing demands is right in the sense that it recognizes work must be limited. But in God's wisdom, entering his rest is the limiter. When we enter this rest—the rest he himself enjoys because his work was very good—work is set in its proper place in our lives.

Practicing sabbath means resting one day and working six days. Working six days is no small ask; it means work is good and something innate to being a human being. Not all six days need to be paid work, and not all work must cease on the Sabbath day, for society and individuals are constantly expending energy to live. It means there is a pattern and rhythm hardwired into humanity, and it should lead us to recognize rest not only as ceasing from the work God has given us to do but also active enjoyment of the work.

Rest as a State of Being

Practicing sabbath is counter-cultural, counter-intuitive, and counter-productive. As Tim Keller and Katherine Leary Alsdorf say, practicing sabbath is a celebration of our design, a declaration of our freedom, and an act of trust.[7] It points us to an ultimate reality that will one day be true.

It may be helpful to consider a little background on the Sabbath. Christ rose from the dead on the first day after the Jewish Sabbath. Alexander Schmemann notes the Sabbath "was not meant to be a 'holy day' opposed to profane ones, a commemoration in time of a past event. Its true meaning was in the transformation of time."[8] R. Paul Stevens, a leading theologian about faith and work, sees "sabbath (the threefold rest of God, human-kind, and creation) as the goal of the salvation story."[9] In addition to the command to practice rest, the Sabbath also points to rest as a state of being available to humanity in Christ now and forever.

However, that does not mean heaven will be about resting as some kind of eternal nap, or that rest as some kind of leisure and self-entertainment on earth is human-ity's greatest reality. Crouch says, "Leisure has sharply diminishing returns, especially when there is no meaningful work ahead of us to which we might apply the insights and energy gained during our year of rest. Image bearers are not meant to take a permanent vacation from responsibility and creativity."[10]

According to Revelation 21, Scripture's vision of heaven is a city coming down to earth. Cities require work. Heaven will have work for us to do. It will be work as God intended: fruitful, fulfilling, and fun. Yet, there will be a state of rest—unhurried, non-anxious rest—the kind of rest that comes when one is fully free, fully known, and fully alive.

That rest is also available today.

In Christ, the people of God can work day to day, hour by hour, in a state of rest, in their identity as God's people. They work to serve him and others, trusting him with the results. It is a true working out of selflessness rather than selfishness. "You are adopted into God's family, so you already have your affirmation. You are justified in God's sight, so you have nothing to prove. You have been saved through a dying sacrifice, so you are free to be a living one. You are loved ceaselessly, so you can work tirelessly in response to a quiet inner fullness," say Keller and Alsdorf.[11]

This is what the writer of Hebrews is getting at in his interpretation of Psalm 95 in Hebrews 3–4. In his commentary on Hebrews, F. F. Bruce says, "This rest which is reserved for the people of God is properly called a 'sabbath rest…' because it is their participation in God's own rest."[12] Hebrews warns those who first put their hope in Christ to remain steadfast in their faith for they could be like Israel after being delivered from slavery. They started well, but they did not remain faithful to the God who delivered them, and that generation did not enter the land of Canaan. "They did not appropriate the good news by faith when they heard it," Bruce says.[13] We, as the people of God today, are urged by the author of Hebrews to enter God's rest. It is open and available.

To enter his rest requires *faith* in Christ, the one who entered God's rest on our behalf and makes it available to us. And it requires *faithfulness* to work and live according to the good work he intended for us to do from before the foundation of the world (Ephesians 2:10).

This means we must learn to trust God with our work and rest practices. Crouch reminds us, "The Creator God is not an idol who extracts endless work while dangling the promise of eventual leisure—he is an abundant

God fully capable of providing everything we need to be faithful to his cosmic pattern of work and rest."[14] Rest builds our trust in God's provision and allows those who work with us or under our authority to rest so they have the opportunity to see God's provision.

And Schmemann exhorts us, "The life that shone forth from the grave was beyond the inescapable limitations of . . . time that leads to death."[15] Death was defeated.

When we work with God and for others in the daily grind, practicing the rhythms of work and rest, we are working and living in the time that leads to true life.

A Framework for Change

JEFF HAANEN AND ROSS CHAPMAN

WE HOPE THAT THE PREVIOUS CHAPTERS have given you a starting point as you reflect on the meaning and purpose of your life's work. We'd like to leave you with the framework we've used to guide all our work here at the Denver Institute for Faith & Work. We believe these five guiding principles paint a picture of what it means to be a redemptive worker, to integrate faith with our daily work. We hope they will be helpful to you as you build a perspective on how your own work is meant to participate in God's redemption and restoration of all aspects of his creation.

The Bible gives us a beautiful picture of the breadth of redemption that heals both our hearts and society. The gospel heals our relationship with God, with ourselves, with others, and with culture itself. God is renewing all things, and we're called to be a part of that mission. Accomplishing this mission calls for a vision that guides our thinking and actions so that we live fully integrated lives—where our private world seamlessly intersects with our public world, and our faith deeply informs not only how we do our work but also the way we develop products and services. This is not a collection of nice phrases. They are biblical principles that become the basis for the hard work of living one's faith in our daily occupations.

A Five-Part Framework

The following five-part framework is designed to influence men and women to make long-term, systemic change that aligns with God's reconciliation mission through their work, and to do so as a person rooted in Christ.

Seek deep spiritual health. Embracing Christ's call to "come follow me" in our work, we actively listen to the Holy Spirit, practice spiritual disciplines, regularly confess our sins, and submit to the sovereignty of God.[1]

Every day we experience a flood of different emotions. Fear, anger, joy, surprise, sadness, disgust, and elation are just some of the emotions we may experience in the course of a day. Our emotional and spiritual health are woven tightly together, yet we often do not regularly and consistently take the time or make the effort to invest in them. Consequently, many of us experience disengagement, addiction, distraction, and mental illness.

But through actively listening to the guidance of the Holy Spirit and practicing spiritual disciplines, we can face our lives honestly without denying reality. We can begin to see God's presence more clearly in the rhythms of our daily work, and this will create a place of emotional and spiritual health where our hearts can experience deep peace.

Think theologically. Embracing the call to be faithful stewards of the mysteries of Christ, we can articulate how Scripture, the historic church, and the gospel of grace influence our work.

In our culture today, there are countless narratives that drive our work: the "isms" (secular humanism, materialism, pantheism, consumerism), the drive for success (status, power, money), and the 300 million plus religions we in America just call "me."

Yet there is one narrative that constantly rises above the noise: the Christian story. It may be obvious, but the first step in integrating faith and work is intentionally asking how Scripture, the historic church, and the gospel of grace influence our work. This covers everything from our motivation to work, our relationships with others, the jobs and projects we choose, the way we spend our careers, and the influence we have in our organizations, communities, and professions. Without this, we literally have no way to understand ourselves, our world, or our culture.

So how can we actually know if we are *thinking theologically*? A simple answer is that our words communicate a real and obvious connection between our thoughts and our actions. The question to ask ourselves is this: What part of God's redemptive history—from Abraham and the call of Israel to Christ and the church in Acts—should influence this decision, right here and right now? How would I articulate and implement it considering the issues before me today?

As we think theologically, realizing the breadth of the gospel for all of life, our theology will move from the merely private sphere to the broader public sphere in witness and service.

Embrace relationships. Embracing the doctrine of the incarnation, we seek to embody love for and toward our work neighbors and to build highly active networks and long-term relationships among peers across sectors.

God cares deeply about relationships. Among all the world religions, the Christian God is the only one who is himself a relationship (Father, Son, and Spirit). The reconciliation of fractured relationships is such a priority for him that God became a man in Christ Jesus so that we might be drawn into the self-giving love of the Trinity. The Bible describes hell as the pain of utter loneliness ("outer darkness") and heaven as a big party ("the wedding supper of the Lamb"). We were made to live in loving relationship—with God and with one another.

If that's true, then the gospel *must* influence our relationships with clients, coworkers, vendors, bosses, patients, students, and everybody in between. How then should we develop redemptive relationships with those we work with?

Where redemptive relationships are not embraced, there is no love and, consequently, no witness. But as we build relationships with others, recognizing that they, too, are made in the image of God, we build broad professional networks and healthy connections rooted in community. This means we place a high value on face-to-face conversations (over merely digital ones), active networks (staying in expects *measurable returns* from what he's entrusted to us; we're not meant to merely get by.

Thus the question becomes, What projects will I undertake today so I can say at the end of the day, "It is good"? Will others join in with me and say about that lesson plan, gas station design, or plate of food, "Indeed, it is good!"? Here is where our work begins to look like the work of God himself.

Serve others sacrificially. Embracing the call to costly discipleship, we value high levels of commitment, acts of sacrificial service, and courageous public witness in all the roles we have.

Embracing the call to justice, we value actions and activities that serve the needs of the poor and marginalized in our work and communities.

Embracing the call to be the body of Christ for the life of the world, we value opportunities to address our most pressing contemporary problems and adopt a broad, interdisciplinary perspective in solving complex issues.

There may be no more common phrase in American business culture than customer service. Yet serve others *sacrificially*? At the center of the Christian faith is Jesus Christ, who sacrificed his life on the cross that others might have eternal life. Are we willing to sacrifice ourselves for the interests of coworkers, bosses, clients, investors, and vendors?

Being a Christian in a pluralistic society will eventually cost us something. It will probably be painful; it may even feel like death. But by serving others sacrificially, we are serving God, our neighbor, and society, honoring his commands to love him and love others. Can we express a courageous public witness, yet always seek to embrace sacrificial service for the well-being of others? Can we put a special value on the needs of the poor and marginalized in our communities? Can we be people of high commitment when everybody else shrinks away—even if it costs us dearly?

In a culture where changing the world has become one of the most common aspirations of graduating college students, we need to hear stories of humble service, good work, and redemptive relationships—all in the context of a story we didn't start and won't finish. We are small. God is big.

Having said that, the body of Christ must not shrink back from the great challenges of our day. We who created the first hospitals in the late Roman Empire; we who established the first universities in the twelfth century;

we who composed sonatas, established economic systems built on virtue, and throughout history defended the worth of *all* men and women as being made in God's image—who are we to shrink back when we see our neighbors in great need today? Countless numbers of people throughout history prepared *both* for acts of great sacrifice *and* deeds of great heroism. We can and must do the same today.

So, what pressing contemporary problems in your organization, community, or profession can be solved through sacrificial service? Who are you gathering across various disciplines to solve these issues? As William Carey once said, how will you "attempt great things for God [and] expect great things from God"? The body of Christ is given as a gift for the life of the world. You and I may be just small cells in Christ's body. But we can gather, we can learn, we can act—and we can be the bearers of a redemption far greater than any one of us individually.

Considering that our time is short, let's focus our efforts on the greatest needs and the known evils of our age. Perhaps then our work might humbly, yet hopefully, point to the redemption of all things in the heavenly Jerusalem,

Acknowledgments

THIS BOOK WAS SHAPED AND CRAFTED out of the work of Denver Institute for Faith & Work, and past and present staff made significant and important contributions to this material. We are particularly grateful to Jeff Haanen, Joanna Meyer, Brian Gray, Dustin Moody, Abby Worland, and Cliff Johnson, who have been key contributors.

Notes

Introduction

[1]Christopher Buchanan, "Chick-fil-A Comes Out on Top of Customer Service Ranking—for the 8th Year," News19, Atlanta, July 2, 2022, www.wltx.com/article/life/food/chickfila-top-customer-service-ranking-8th-year/101-a365663e-1a6d-4891-ad08-0b01a5a8f02a.

[2]Dorothy L. Sayers, "Why Work?," in *Letters to a Diminished Church: Passionate Arguments for the Relevance of Christian Doctrine* (Nashville, TN: W Publishing Group, 2004), 131.

1: The Importance of Work

[1]Pope Francis, *Fratelli Tutti (On Fraternity and Social Friendship)*, (Rome: Libreria Editrice Vaticana), 162, www.vatican.va/content/francesco/en/encyclicals/documents/papa-francesco_20201003_enciclica-fratelli-tutti.html.

[2]Max Weber, *The Sociology of Religion* (Boston, MA: Beacon Press, 1993), 270.

[3]Greg Ayers, "New Research Shows More Pastors Are Preaching about Faith and Work. How Are People in the Pews Being Impacted by This Change?," March 4, 2015, Institute for Faith, Work

& Economics, https://tifwe.org/more-pastors-are-preaching-about
-faith-and-work/.

[4]A. W. Tozer, *The Pursuit of God: The Human Thirst for the Divine* (1948;
repr., Chicago, IL: Moody Publishers, 2015), 56.

[5]Lesslie Newbigin, *Truth to Tell: The Gospel as Public Truth* (Grand
Rapids, MI: Eerdmans, 1991), 2.

[6]This section is lightly adapted from "Servant & Witness: John Stott
and the DIFW Mission," https://denverinstitute.org/servant-witness
-john-stott-and-the-difw-mission/, ©Denver Institute for Faith &
Work and used with permission.

[7]John Stott, *Christian Mission in the Modern World* (Downers Grove, IL:
IVP Academic, 1975), 31-32.

3: Created and Placed by God for Good Work

[1]Helmut Thielicke, *Being Human . . . Becoming Human: An Essay in
Christian Anthropology* (New York: Doubleday Books, 1984), 46.

4: The Reality of Work and Calling

[2]Os Guinness, *The Call: Finding and Fulfilling the Central Purpose of Your
Life* (Nashville, TN: Thomas Nelson, 2003), 31.

5: Work in a Politicized and Polarized Society

[1]Barna, "A New Generation Expresses its Skepticism and Frustration
with Christianity," Research Releases in Millennials & Generations,
September 21, 2007, www.barna.com/research/a-new-generation
-expresses-its-skepticism-and-frustration-with-christianity/.

[2]Some content in this section is ©Denver Institute for Faith & Work
and used with permission.

[3]Reinhold Niebuhr, *Christian Realism and Political Problems* (New York:
Scribner, 1953), 116.

6: Monday Through Saturday Missionaries

[1]Some content in this chapter is from "Why Work Is at the Heart of God's Mission," https://denverinstitute.org/why-work-is-at-the-heart-of-gods-mission/, ©Denver Institute for Faith & Work and used with permission.

[2]Darrell L. Guder, et al., *The Missional Church: A Vision for the Sending of the Church in North America* (Grand Rapids, MI: William B. Eerdmans, 1998), 102.

[3]Elton Trueblood, *The Common Ventures of Life: Marriage, Birth, Work and Death* (New York: Harper & Brothers, 1949), 87.

[4]Lesslie Newbigin, *Foolishness to the Greeks: The Gospel and Western Culture* (Grand Rapids, MI: Eerdmans, 1986), 143.

[5]Robert N. Bellah, et al, *Habits of the Heart: Individualism and Commitment in American Life* (Berkeley, CA: University of California Press, 1985), 287-88.

[6]Dorothy L. Sayers, "Why Work?" in *Letters to a Diminished Church: Passionate Arguments for the Relevance of Christian Doctrine* (Nashville, TN: Thomas Nelson, 2004), 127-28.

[7]Sayers, "Why Work?," 118.

7: Rest for and in the Working

[1]Alexandra Kalev and Frank Dobbin, "The Surprising Benefits of Work/Life Support," *Harvard Business Review Magazine*, September-October 2022 issue, https://hbr.org/2022/09/the-surprising-benefits-of-work-life-support.

[2]Timothy Keller and Katherine Leary Alsdorf, *Every Good Endeavor: Connecting Your Work to God's Work* (New York: Penguin, 2012), 227.

[3]Will Messenger, ed., *Theology of Work Bible Commentary, Volume 1: Genesis through Deuteronomy* (Peabody, MA: Hendrickson, 2015), 98.

[4]Messenger, *Theology of Work Bible Commentary*, 98.

[5]Keller and Alsdorf, *Every Good Endeavor*, 229-30.

[6]Andy Crouch, *Playing God* (Downers Grove, IL: InterVarsity Press, 2013), 254.

[7]Keller and Alsdorf, *Every Good Endeavor*, 235-36.

[8]Alexander Schmemann, *For the Life of the World: Sacraments and Orthodoxy* (Crestwood, NY: St. Vladimir's Seminary Press), 51.

[9]R. Paul Stevens, *The Other Six Days: Vocation, Work, and Ministry in Biblical Perspective* (Grand Rapids, MI: Eerdmans, 1999), 37-38.

[10]Crouch, *Playing God*, 259.

[11]Keller and Alsdorf, *Every Good Endeavor*, 233.

[12]F. F. Bruce, *The Epistle to the Hebrews, Revised*, The New International Commentary on the New Testament (Grand Rapids, MI: Eerdmans, 1990), 109.

[13]Bruce, *The Epistle to the Hebrews*, 109.

[14]Crouch, *Playing God*, 261-62.

[15]Schmemann, *For the Life of the World*, 51.

Epilogue

[1]Originally published online, Denver Institute for Faith & Work, "Guiding Principles," accessed April 3, 2023, www.denverinstitute .org/guiding-principles, ©Denver Institute for Faith & Work and used with permission.

Further Reading

The Call: Finding and Fulfilling the Central Purpose of Your Life, Os Guinness, (Nashville, TN: W Publishing Group, 1998).

The Economics of Neighborly Love: Investing in Your Community's Compassion and Capacity, Tom Nelson (Downers Grove, IL: InterVarsity Press, 2017).

Every Good Endeavor: Connecting Your Work to God's Work, Timothy Keller with Katherine Leary Alsdorf (New York: Penguin, 2014).

Kingdom Calling: Vocational Stewardship for the Common Good, Amy L. Sherman (Downers Grove, IL: InterVarsity Press, 2011).

Redeeming Work: A Guide to Discovering God's Calling for Your Career, Bryan J. Dik (West Conshohocken, PA: Templeton Press, 2020).

Surprised by Hope: Rethinking Heaven, the Resurrection, and the Mission of the Church, N. T. Wright (New York: HarperCollins, 2008).

Theology of Work Bible Commentary, Theology of Work Project, William Messenger, ed., 5 vols. (Peabody, MA: Hendrickson, 2015).

Visions of Vocation: Common Grace for the Common Good, Steven Garber (Downers Grove, IL: InterVarsity Press, 2014).

Vocation: The Setting for Human Flourishing, Michael Berg (Irvine, CA: New Reformation, 2020).

"Why Work?" Dorothy L. Sayers in *Letters to a Diminished Church: Passionate Arguments for the Relevance of Christian Doctrine* (Nashville, TN: W Publishing Group, 2004).

Women, Work, and Calling: Step into Your Place in God's World, Joanna Meyer (Downers Grove, IL: InterVarsity Press, 2023).

Work Matters: Connecting Sunday Worship to Monday Work, Tom Nelson (Wheaton, IL: Crossway, 2011).

Work Matters: Lessons from Scripture, R. Paul Stevens (Grand Rapids, MI: W. B. Eerdmans, 2012).

Work: The Meaning of Your Life, A Christian Perspective, second ed., Lester DeKoster (Grand Rapids, MI: Christian's Library, 1982).

Working from the Inside Out: A Brief Guide to Inner Work That Transforms Our Outer World, Jeff Haanen (Downers Grove, IL: InterVarsity Press, 2023).

ABOUT DENVER INSTITUTE FOR FAITH & WORK

denver
institute
FOR FAITH & WORK

Over a lifetime, most of us will spend more than ninety thousand hours at work, but we often miss what God has to say about work's purpose and mission. Because society lacks a compelling vision and purpose for work, we endeavor to see people formed for mission with God in their daily work for the transformation of workplaces, professions, industries, and cities. We believe individuals, families, and communities thrive when people envision their daily work as an opportunity to join God in his work to make all things new. In our public engagement initiatives, we help people live with God, for the world, through their daily work. Some of our nationally-focused initiatives include *The Faith & Work Podcast*, the *Teach Us to Pray Podcast*, CityGate Fellowships, books and articles available on our website, and Women, Work & Calling.

Learn more at **www.denverinstitute.org**
and find us on social media **@DenverInstitute**.

Also from Denver Institute for Faith & Work

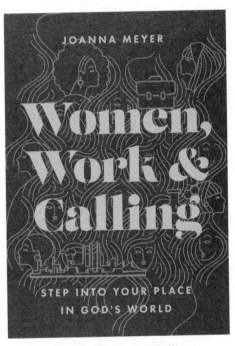

Women, Work, and Calling
978-1-5140-0793-8